ACROSTIC
WOODSTOCK

ACROSTIC
WOODSTOCK

Dear Miriam,

For your help with these

Poems and for your good company,

I thank you!

With best wishes,

POEMS BY
WILL NIXON

Will Nixon 12-10-15

ACKNOWLEDGMENTS

Some of these poems first appeared in the "Poet's Corner" in the *Woodstock Times*. *Rattle* published "National Poetry Month" online.

Suggestions from friends have made these poems stronger. Thank you Peter Wallace, Alison Koffler, Jana Martin, Suzanne Bennett, Amanda Gulla, Bibi Wein, Bob Fisher, Scott Anderson, Violet Snow, Miriam Ben-Yaacov, and Nancy Kline.

Thank you Michael Perkins for being my partner at Bushwhack Books. Thank you Saul Bennett for living in my memory.

Acrostic Woodstock. Copyright ©2015 by Will Nixon.

Published by Bushwhack Books
www.bushwhackbooks.com

Printed in the United States of America

Acrostic Woodstock : poems / by Will Nixon.
[Woodstock, NY] : Bushwhack Books, 2015.
p. 86 : ill : cm.
ISBN: 978-0-9886398-4-3
1. Woodstock (N.Y.)- History. 2. Woodstock (N.Y.)- Guidebooks. 3. Poetry- American.
974.734
F129 .W85

Illustrations © 2015 by Carol Zaloom
Cover & book design by Melissa Mykal Batalin

Everything is astonishing.
If it doesn't seem that way,
keep looking until it does.
　　　　　—Michael Perkins

CONTENTS

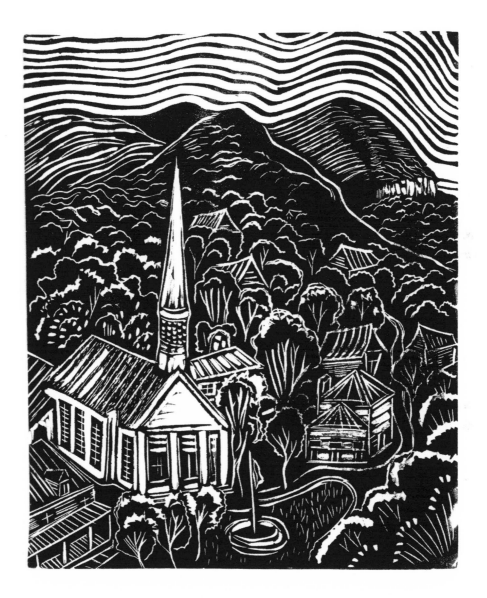

In 1996, I left my midtown apartment and my marriage for a new life in a Catskills log cabin. I hadn't fallen out of love, but my wife was a lifelong Manhattanite who'd never learned how to drive and thought of the suburbs as "the country," while I'd burned out on city life. I'd once been a Boy Scout, a college ski bum, and a backpacker, and now that I was nearing forty, I was an environmental journalist, an avid day hiker, and a late-blooming nature writer heeding the call of the wild. As I later wrote in a poem:

MOVING INTO MY CABIN

Hung a Cherokee bear mask by the door.
Loaded the pencil holder with wild turkey feathers.
Gathered an armload of dead branches
for the kindling box. Picked asters and goldenrod
for the old pickling jar on the table.
Decorated the windowsill with birch bark
and bird nests, a littered shotgun shell
for a humorous touch. Swept mouse droppings
off the shelves. Shook dust from the fireplace rug.
Noticed again the smell of the cabin:
thirty-year-old logs varnished whiskey brown,
charred chimney stones, wool blankets
passed from owner to owner.

Brewed pine needle tea. Wiped owl pellets
from the porch bench. Transcribed in my journal
the song of the stream. Listened to the red-eyed vireo
owning his treetop till sunset. Lingered
over sauteed mushrooms and stew.
Studied moths on the windows,
dozens, hundreds, fluttering, crawling,
staring with eyes tinier than crumbs, yet gold,
gold as fire. Stepped outside to join moths
at the windows, my first friends.

The magic didn't last. After five years the cabin had become as familiar as any other live-in workspace, but with a woodstove that leaked smoke puffs like a cigarette and mice that ran rampant and mold and a bath drain that froze into an ice plug, leaving me to scoop buckets of dirty shower water into the toilet to empty the tub. The pièce de résistance may have been the frozen toilet bowl that cracked open like a porcelain egg in my plumber's arms as he carried it out the door. He'd gotten to know me too well. My Thoreauvian romance with solitude had ended. I'd fallen in love with a woman who invited me to share her home by cornfields south of the Catskills. I could now appreciate having a thermostat on the wall in place of a woodstove. Alas, our relationship foundered, and when I moved out, I wanted to get back to the mountains.

I looked at several cabins, moldy and expensive. Then, descending into Woodstock on a mountain road, I had a radical idea: why not live in town? By then I knew that the curse of country living was that in order to do anything social I had to drive for half an hour first. And didn't I come to Woodstock all the time for Pilates or poetry readings? The side streets had cute cottages. Within days I found a homey French country-like cottage beside a stream, yet a few minutes walk from the village green. My landlady often rode the bus from the city to stay in her own tiny bungalow in back, cantilevered over the stream on a metal stilt. Seated at a picture window, she practiced her electric piano, pursuing beginner's lessons in her sixties. On New Year's Eve she invited me to join for an apéritif with her twin sister visiting from the city for an before I went my way and they stayed in to watch *Mulholland Drive*. How could I not love Woodstock with them as my emissaries?

My first morning in town, I walked to breakfast, something I hadn't done since living in Manhattan. The curse of the car was over. Many days I didn't drive at all, not for groceries, office supplies, or even the movies down the road at Tinker Street Cinema. Woodstock was that rare upstate village built for pedestrians. I regularly ran into someone I knew for a sidewalk conversation, the chance encounters that foster a sense of community. Some saw Woodstock as a tourist mecca living off its tie-dye reputation, but I enjoyed being a bit of a tourist myself. At Candlestock I treated myself to exotic candles to burn at my desk as a writing ritual. At the Golden Notebook I browsed new poetry volumes. Seated on Taco Juan's bench with my iced cappuccino, I people-watched the visiting hordes and had as much fun—maybe more—as I'd once had birding with binoculars from my cabin porch. One Sunday I even joined the drummers on the village green, putting aside my lifelong embarrassment at having a poor sense of rhythm. Amid the veteran drummers and casual drop-ins, I could pound away to my heart's content. The Woodstock motto, as I'd learned, was that you're never too old to have a happy childhood.

Several weeks after settling in, I dropped in on a press event held by the Woodstock Land Conservancy to announce a campaign to protect Overlook Mountain, which rises above the village like our version of Mount Rushmore. If this weekday event hadn't been a short walk around the corner in town, I wouldn't have taken the time to go, though as a journalist I'd once covered conservation in the Adirondacks, so the subject was dear to my heart. That I was no longer a reporter didn't bother the WLC. Before I knew it, I'd been recruited to join their Overlook committee, then a year later I joined the board. In Woodstock, I discovered, you didn't need a fancy resumé, you simply needed a willingness to show up and participate. Later I served as a library trustee. I acted in a play for the first time in my life. I read poems on the radio. As a small town Woodstock offered opportunities I wouldn't have imagined for myself in Manhattan or at my wilderness cabin.

Most surprisingly of all, I became a Woodstock author. One night at a wine and cheese gathering to read the poetry of Hart Crane, who'd visited the art colony in 1923 as a young enthusiast for literature and hard cider, Michael Perkins and I decided to walk across the town and write about our adventures for the *Woodstock Times*. Michael had moved upstate in the early seventies and had already written several short histories about the parade of characters drawn to the town from its start as a wilderness outpost through its rise as an arts colony. Hearing his tales, I caught the history bug myself. In time, we gathered our essays into *Walking Woodstock: Journeys into the Wild Heart of America's Most Famous Small Town*, which became a local bestseller. Then we did *The Pocket Guide to Woodstock* for visitors. Without intending to, I'd become something of an expert on the place.

On a retreat in Maine, I began a ritual of writing an acrostic poem as a whimsical warm-up exercise before getting down to the serious work of the day. I picked a random phrase for a title, which I also wrote down the margin as the first letter for each line. Then I filled in the lines, favoring spontaneity over coherence. I had fun writing gibberish. Yet I intrigued myself at times by producing a string of words that almost made sense. They weren't my typical poems, but I liked them.

After my retreat, I was due to participate in a reading for Michael Perkins's latest book, a collection of aphorisms. Inspired to compose a serious acrostic poem, I wrote "Michael Perkins, Poet" to read at the event. Alas, a week beforehand, Michael fell and broke his hip. His friends stepped in to read his work before a packed house at the Woodstock library, but Michael missed everything in his hospital bed. So I visited to read him my poem while he lay propped up on pillows. The dampness in his eyes told me all I needed to know about poetry and friendship. I gave him a framed copy to place by his bedside. More than once I'd sworn off poetry because the public was so indifferent to the form, but now I knew that poetry had a purpose. Rather than writing for acclaim, I'd write for the people who mattered in my life.

Soon afterward, I brought copies of *The Pocket Guide to Woodstock* to a gift shop in town. The manager asked me to sign them, which I was happy to do. "Enjoy Woodstock!" I wrote in the book, followed by my signature. "Enjoy Woodstock!" five times over. By the time I got home I was itching to try the phrase as an acrostic poem. The result surprised me. I decided to see how much of this town I could put into poems.

ENJOY
WOODSTOCK

Enter a
Nation without a name.
Join the
Occupation of
Yelling with ridiculous joy.

We all need
Other versions of
Ourselves.
Don't believe the
Shadows or the
Tributes.
Only
Certainty can
Kill your crazy dreams.

H. HOUST & SON

Heaven and
Hell in the same aisle as the helium balloons you buy to knock some sense into the sky.
Oil for the paraffin lamp so you can write poems by the light Emily wrote by.
Umber for the moods too much like March you begin to miss by July.
Suppose you weren't born with the genes for splicing wires or hanging chandeliers.
There's still hope at the hardware. The same two clowns who manage this place, the General
& the Saboteur, also happen to manage your psyche. One never fails. The other always has fun.
So buy the dog bone shaped like an Olmec god. The squirrel-proof bird feeder that squirrels prefer.
Order the ¼" *screwlatchboltswitch* that only costs 39¢ whatever the hell it's for.
Nobody votes against hardware. Rumor says there's a light bulb in back that burns forever.

CATSKILL ART & OFFICE SUPPLY

Charcoal is best for darkness and light.
Angels appear from the copy machine.
Temptations are best framed in gold or red.
Sympathy cards aren't true, nor should they be.
Knuckleheads may play with the skeleton standing
In the corner meant for an art class, but I say,
Let them find bliss with street chalk's 36 colors.
Let them wallow in tie-dye or the volcano-making kit.
Art should do more than flatter fields with sunlight.
Rough up your canvas. Glue sticks serve a purpose.
Tracing paper can still capture the invisible spirit.
&
Once you've lost the X on your treasure map
Find the manager with hair dyed like a traffic cone to ask if the
Future is like mist from a spray can or does pandemonium look better
In glitter? Ask if round brushes are best for the void.
Cancer will not be solved by the lab rats.
Early humans painted deep in the caves and far into the desert.
Somewhere their truth remains true. Calendars promise
Us 365 empty white squares not to be wasted.
Primrose no longer depends upon flowers.
Primrose can be found in encaustics or angelic choirs.
Laughter definitely comes in spray cans. I dare
You to draw a god that isn't yourself with better eyebrows.

CATSKILL MOUNTAIN PIZZA

Can't stop:
Anchovies, applesauce, ants,
Toppings piled higher than haystacks,
Sausages fatter than baseball bats and
Knishes trucked up from Queens.
I've got an appetite to eat a
Little bit of the moon while I'm at it.
Let's order sides:
Marshmallows, mayhem, blue M&Ms.
Once I'm finished you'll
Understand. I've got a hole in my heart that
Needs to be filled. Licorice sticks, cookie dough ice cream,
Taco pommes frites. Hot sauce galore to make your
Asshole feel like a volcano—oh, my dear Lord!
Indigestion be damned. But
Nothing can top a
Plain pizza pie. So let's just sit here, you and
I watching the girls go by with
Zebra-striped tans from their bra straps. Pity the poor
Zombies who taste nothing but brains. I've got an
Appetite for the world with everything on it.

SUNFLOWER NATURAL FOODS

Soaps alone, a
United
Nations of scents to re-
Fresh me from the check-out line's weary patience:
Lavender,
Oatmeal, goats' milk, shea butter, Dead Sea minerals and mud.
When I hold one then another to my nostrils, I become an
Egyptian, a
Roman, a Rumanian, hell, a
Neanderthal who baptized himself a believer in all things:
Angels, tornadoes, the moon that blushed red.
The bathtub I want will be bluestone
Under a waterfall as hard as a symphony after the
Rain. I'll submerge to my neck and my knees, and I'll shed
All of this dirt from digging graves for myself. I'll
Lather and travel the world via my nose,
French cathedrals to coconut islands.
Only when my fingertips turn into prunes,
Only when my calluses soften to joy on my toes
Do I dare say I've washed off the
Scars of regret.

LANDAU GRILL & BAR

Leather-clad, wing-eating champions
Assembled from Ramapo, Mahwah, points south,
Nam Knights or not, a pound of wind in their beards,
Drawn by crispy shrimp and burgers that bleed in the hands,
Assembled from sheet rockers, welders, towering crane operators,
Until Sunday night they've got full tanks and all the time in the world.

Great riders understand ghosts in their mirrors. Great
Riders know innocence never had a rest stop.
Instead they drink amber pints and
Laugh at the fears they've left behind. The
Long days of summer have yet to break any promises,

& I, eavesdropping with my salmon
Burger and balsamic salad, wonder what I've
Avoided, having never
Ridden or washed my face in the road's roaring fate.

PEGASUS FOOTWEAR

Pegasus, tell me, did you bother with Birkenstocks or
Earth Shoes when you commanded your gas station empire?
Galoshes reserved for the muck and the mire.
Alligator boots never lived up to their promise.
Sandals were for saints I didn't want to be. Pegasus,
Uggs ask their men to take out the garbage in the snow.
Sheep skin slippers nurse the fat lady's ingrown nails and corns.
Flames, that's what I want on my feet, the traction to leap
Over the moon and chase Jaguars down the highways you
Once ruled, bold as high octane and cheap as a $2 kiss.
Tell me you're not just a souvenir sign on the back wall.
We should team up to fly Quixote-like at the stars. Leave
Earth to the tread marks of the deskbound and the debt collectors.
As we kick through the clouds, we'll teach patience to the
Rain and free the sky from remorse. I lace up my fliers to join you.

MARILYN CRISPELL
SOLO PIANO

May your fingers
Arrest mayhem even if
Riots spread from your pinkies. May
Interludes arrive fresh from the moon. May you
Lead this cacophony up and down the keyboard into
Your moment of silence
Not so different from the spell
Cast by a spruce tree laden with snow
Right before the branches let go with an *oomph*.
I've heard
So much in your music that a piano can't
Play, the toe tapping of dinosaurs, the
Elves slurping milk, the bell towers dancing a jig.
Listen, the keys are starting to avalanche.
Lady, ski them like an angel.

MICHAEL PERKINS, POET

May your
Itching feet be
Cured by the
Holy waters after parting the
Angry tides. May the good
Earth
Leave you with
Plenty of room to prosper and
Escape with your contentment. May you
Replace the
Known with the
Incomprehensible
Not because you're
Suspicious, but because you
Propose to
Open the tomb of
Eternity to release the Lord's most
Ticklish feathers.

MIKHAIL HOROWITZ
STANDUP POET

Mad hatter,

Insolent

Kvetch and

Hubristic lampoonist.

Already

I've exhausted my vocabulary. Isn't

Laughter a kosher aphrodisiac? Or did I already say that?

Hadassah has banned me from cruise ships. But I promise you, no

Octopus was harmed in the making of this Bar Mitzvah video.

Rugelach rapture in Ramallah: let's rock 'n' roll, baby! No

Opinion is too low, but we do need a spell check.

When we've finished here

I'll

Treat you to gurus in tutus.

Zee end is nigh! My next act is spinach pie.

SPARROW

Saintly, bearded, baseball-capped progenitor of one-word Neanderthal
Poetry. Perennial candidate with kasha in Tupperware for bus rides.
Arbiter of crossed wires and Zen koans rehabbed as Letters to the Editor.
Righteous, last-in-line follower of laugh riots, dressed as himself for Halloween.
Ready-made pagan savior awaiting his lost tribe of oak village gnomes—
Oh, Sparrow,
Why do I still see you as an owl speaking through Walt Whitman's beard?

NORTH COUNTRY POETS

Not like you
Or I who
Revel in
Tulip trees and magnolias,
Hermits almost,
Close cousins to Eskimos, eyebrows like
Owls,
Underwear smelling of chainsaws. They
Need little
Training in silence. They
Remember every unspoken slight.
You see them at
Poetry readings, the
Ones who never take off their wool hats, not
Even when
The
Saints promise spring.

NATIONAL POETRY MONTH

Nobody's fooled.
April is tax month, the month you take off your snow
Tires, the month moths rediscover your windows.
It was the cruelest month for Eliot, but he lived in England.
One
Night in the rain the salamanders crawl out to be slaughtered,
All of their pink-meat road smorgasbord eaten by dawn.
Laughter sounds its most brutal in crows. No,

Poetry isn't a hymnal
Or a wish list for the soul. It's definitely not the
Eggs hidden by the Easter Bunny. But it is a legitimate
Tax deduction, a money-losing pursuit the I
RS doesn't question. Poor poetry:
Yesterday's news still hoping to be relevant for tomorrow.

Math, now that's worth teaching the whole year, especially
Online. Algorithms, that's where today's genius lies.
Nobody will condemn you for poetry, but
To let it go on for more than a month,
Hey, that's a little bit of insanity.

COLONY CAFÉ

Cold enough for the
Open mic poets to declaim to the yule log. Cold enough for the
Last of the Basquiat imitators to decorate this Moroccan hall. Cold enough for my
Old friend, Saul, to join me onstage in a rubber Richard
Nixon mask while I recite Halloween poems. Cold enough for a group
Yelp at the moon as the werewolf emerges from us all.
Cold enough to count your fingers in blessing
At leading so many lives. Cold enough to accept that almost all poetry
Fails in the end, but never quite cold
Enough to close.

COLONY OF THE ARTS

Cultivating creativity, everyone given an
Opportunity: napkin poets, cornfield painters, the
Librarian who does stand-up about soggy bathtub books.
One
Night at the Colony Café, an aging Dadaist, whom
You'd know if I named him, climbed through a window in a frog mask in the midst
Of my Halloween reading, upstaging me, infuriating me, causing me to think,
Fuck Woodstock, I've had it with the wannabes treating the arts as cheap
Therapy; this town doesn't deserve serious poetry. The problem is,
He's all I remember, the guy flopping into the room in a frog mask as if to say
Enough is enough, you're drowning me with your pathetic laments and
Asinine odes to your toenails. Yes, I should admit genius when I see it, not in my
Reading about the metaphorical meaning of masks, but in the impulse
To do something disruptive and weird. He
Stood up and could have seen a roomful of tropical fish, but, instead, settled for us.

YOUR BOX OF CRAYONS

Yawning, yelling, yodeling, signing your barbaric yawp, your life
Onstage
Under my direction will not be a dress
Rehearsal for charm school or a desperate hunt for applause.
Bravery won't make you into a hero, nor will seducing the blonde.
Of all the colors in your box of crayons, yellow makes you most human.
X-rated or not, you can't be a transvestite without a jealous heart.
Of all the things you're burning to say, let me just say,
Forget about the speech to your mother. Focus on the lampshade in the
Corner if you intend to play the perfect drag queen.
Remember, *The Lady in Question* is not who she seems:
All of her smiles also come in poison. So be like the coyotes
Yipping and yowling at the edge of the night.
Of all the feelings you haven't yet shared, from orange to blue,
None can ever be worn down to a
Stub. You have twenty-four crayons. Now show us.

DONALD FAGEN, ASSHOLE

Don't be an asshole.
Or be an asshole, but don't be a scold.
Nobody begrudges you living on Dylan's estate.
All the creeps in your songs, I
Loved them too, Katy, Snake Mary, Chino, and
Doctor Wu. I must have
Friended you in
Another age of extremes.
Gone now, Kid Charlemagne,
Everyone's favorite acid guru.
Nobody remembers
Annandale quite the way you do. I'm a
Sucker for reunions at which the band plays "My Old
School" even though I failed to paint my face like all the rest.
Here we are growing
Old, but you still sound pure and
Lonely on the radio, young
Enough to celebrate your very own disgrace.

THE CENTER FOR PHOTOGRAPHY

The room upstairs with
Hammers on the wall where Dylan typed poems while
Evading his bratty reputation down the road,
Can I go there? Can I
Elope with his genius for kissing off failures?
Nobody cared about Robert Zimmerman, least of all him.
The Dylanologists will tell you, instead, of his days in the White Room upstairs.
Enough with idolatry, you might say, but I'd
Rather
Fancy Ginsberg in the swimming pool playing
Octopus with his brains, while Albert Grossman writes checks with a
Rattlesnake scrawl, and Dylan feels lonely upstairs in the belly of his whale.
Please don't tell me time marches on.
Here
On
The gallery walls hang photographs
Of the
Gray chaos of tree branches and vines
Reminding us that nature's intelligence looks like an unraveling brain.
All those afternoons Dylan sat typing Beatnik
Poetry in preparation for whatever came next—like a song—
He paid no heed to practical life.
You know, this guy will never get out of your hair.

MICHAEL LANG, MUSIC PROMOTER

Man of mystery, out scouting
In Tannersville, plotting, perhaps?
Curly-haired puckish impresario, why is
He here in *this* hamlet eagerly painting itself
A new future for tourists, each Victorian storefront
Elated in Caribbean orange or periwinkle, un-
Like Woodstock, preserved colonial and white.
Let me guess; he's
Alone on his phone at the patio table in
Need of launching something new.
Gone, long gone, Woodstock '69, even '94.
Maybe Tannersville '18 can re-
Unite the tribes.
Still, the sidewalks are empty, and
I'm bored by the soap and peppermint
Country Store, though a taxidermy shop offers a
Promethea moth framed in black I'm tempted to buy;
Rebels should fly across the night with eyes on their wings.
Once Michael Lang was a shirtless wonder in a leather vest on his
Motorcycle at the festival he spawned, preternaturally calm in a sea of mud.
Once I was too young to understand what he'd done.
The improbable Mets had discovered how to win, and
Eighth-grade English beckoned with *The Grapes of Wrath*.
Rock 'n' roll wasn't my religion then, but the girl in red surely was.

TINKER STREET CINEMA

The old Methodist church
Is the Tinker Street Cinema
Now, but the sermons haven't changed:
Knowledge without love is a loaded gun,
Empathy is both what kills us and keeps us alive.
Righteous indignation may pay well for an evening, but
Spare us moralizing, like bathrooms marked "Night" and "Day."
They both look the same inside. The real
Revelation is that you and the hero feel the same,
Even if he's named Brian Wilson and hears voices in the table forks,
Even as a rock star trying to make cellos saw the moon in half.
There's nothing in *Love & Mercy* you don't understand.
Christ didn't appear, but Jimi Hendrix did on this very stage
In 1969, the
Night he jammed "The Star-Spangled Banner" the week before his
Encore brought duende down to the cow pastures of the Aquarian Age.
May he rest in peace, this fringe-jacketed shaman who made a left-handed
Anthem out of the war for our soul so young and uninsured.

AT LEVON'S GRAVE

An Arkansas flag and a guitar pick cut from a bank card.
Two dozen weathered drum sticks bunched in a fish bowl.

Let me say, I wasn't a fan until that night I saw your smile
Emerge like ivory in the blue light at a Midnight Ramble.
Very few must have known how close you were to the end.
Once you sat at your drums the roadhouse blues resumed,
Not a lick out of tune, perfect, too perfect for me, but your
Smile hovered like an angel wiser than I was, light-winged,

Grandfatherly, as freely given as candy, undaunted by age,
Ready to be shared wherever the winds of the heart blew.
After the show it wasn't yet midnight, but I didn't linger. I
Ventured out to follow my headlights as wide as your grin.
Everywhere else the black forest swallowed the starlight.

L.L. BEAN FREE SHIPPING

Larry?
Louie? Have you
Been sending me catalogs of men more handsome than I'll
Ever be, standing tall
And plaid by the Christmas tree? Their blond labs
Never steal cookies from the plate, do they? Speaking for my
Feet, yes, I'd like to start the day in your Shearling Slippers, then when I'm
Ready to go out, how about your Snow Sneakers in Slate Gray or Dark Cement?
Every page lists colors I didn't know had a name.
Every plaid probably has a bloody history back in
Scotland, but we needn't go into that now.
Here's the perfect Christmas wreath, and here's the perfect family snowshoeing
In the
Perfect snow.
Perhaps you don't know, but
I don't have a family or the perfect wife, so I
Need the monogrammed plaid sleeping bag like I need a plugged
Gopher hole, which is to say, not a lot, but just a little.

SNOWPLOW

Saint of sand and grit.
No nonsense scraper of cold truths.
On the job at any hour with a crooked smile.
We await your releasing us from cottage solitude.
Perhaps the Romans conquered civilizations, and the
Lexus SUVs on TV plow their
Own wings of snow, but we trust you.
We listen for the arrival of your rough prayers.

THE POTHOLE SEASON

They shovel cold asphalt, these
He-men from County Highway, after frost heaves have
Eaten plenty more face-sized
Pits filled with puddles
On Glasco's grubby shoulders. It's the season. Maybe
They could fill a
Hole
Of mine: the night
Last week I dreamed of my late wife,
Emma, now inviting me to
Stay over in her apartment of ashes.
Emma, how many times have I said goodbye? It's
Almost March and the
Sky this afternoon hurts with blue the way love should. I
Open someone's mailbox just to see what message this walk holds—or
No I don't, but I wave at the county guys and say—but I don't know what to say.

COOPER LAKE TRESPASSING

Calling upon the Cooper Lake Whale I
Once saw on a March morning when loons pleaded
Overhead and water spouted tall and proud by the far end, a
Perfectly natural fountain I've never seen again, I
Ease along the shoreline to my chosen
Rock to sit and wait, alas,
Like in *The National Enquirer* for a miracle.
A skeptic, loveless again, I
Know the Cooper Lake Whale doesn't
Exist any more than Bigfoot out in Shandaken or
The long-tailed mountain lions everyone claims to see.
Really, all I can honestly report is a thinning fog
Easing off the pewter lake surface, its calm
Stillness now ruffled by a breeze.
Perhaps I have only myself to blame.
All my life I've wanted to be
Special, a keeper of great
Secrets, but now
I know what everyone knows: you
Need to create your own
Gods, even a whale waiting years between breaths.

SUNFROST HALLOWEEN

Such sad smiling pirates, the pumpkins don't
Understand their
Newly carved faces or why they must give up their seeds
For Halloween. They
Remember golden days in the field rows, an
Orange army growing bigger and bolder under the tireless
Sun. They didn't believe they'd ever reach
Terminal plumpness or their brethren would become pies.

Here, I swear, I once saw Che Guevara's carved face
Alight and defiant with savage eyebrows and revolutionary beret,
Liberating, or planning to, his hundred brethren
Lined up on the farm stand shelves: witches, warlocks,
Owls, Santa Claus, ET, and Richard Nixon with a phallic nose.
When the wind stirred and tricked their candle flames
Every one but two winked and returned, a pledge to
Endure until the wax ran out. Che Guevara still burned,
Never one to fear the night or the hollowness inside.

CHAINSAW BEAR

Crudely carved totem of the country weekender,
Heedless before carpenter ants, porch guardian to 20,000 books inside,
Amanuensis is his name—scribe, muse, joker, alterego with wooden teeth and nut brown eyes.
In the past his ancestors claimed a place in the stars, a past so long ago his ancestors still had tails.
Now we have mythologists to explain what can't be explained about the minds of bears.
Seven feet tall with a grin or a grimace that could house a hornet's nest,
Amanuensis is the centerpiece of porch cocktail parties
Without saying a word, the guardian of 20,000
Books inside, a private library of the famous and forgotten. He knows
Everything about Goldilocks, Jim Beam, and backwoods Tennessee. This winter he'll stand once
Again in his ragged cloak of snow
Remembering dreamy days of hibernation before shamans stole his medicine.

HOTEL RUINS

Happy, honest gossips of wind and rain, the ghostly
Occupants prefer meteors to window shades or chandeliers.
They listen to birch trees deliver Sunday sermons in the parlor.
Enlightened porcupines take attendance by the door. No longer do they chew
Luggage handles for the salt. Wouldn't you rather be married in these
Ruins, where ferns allow no other perfumes? The chimney
Understands the babble of the swifts nesting up and down its throat.
It's fun to climb the ballroom stairs to the open air for the waltzing butterflies.
Nobody remembers the Irish maids or the stubborn mule. The rattle-
Snakes are doing just fine. You can dance to their maraca tails.

FIBERFLAME

Freedom gets
In your hair. The song on the radio
Beats you to your own sadness before you're out of the driveway.
Eating glue isn't the
Right idea, not for the kids, not for you. So try something new.
Fiberflame has boxes of fabrics and buttons that must hold a clue. Remember the gold
Lamé David Bowie wore when life was so gay?
All of these boxes must hold the scraps of somebody's genius.
Maybe you were meant to paint a frog on a dinner plate or sew buttons for a haiku.
Even the children are drawing themselves with earth-shaking shoes.

DRUMMING CIRCLE

Deeper than your heartbeat dares to go,
Rumbling your psyche tamed by the radio,
Undermining melodies taught by timid trolls,
Making mountains echo and village traffic slow,
Making drummers into kingpins dropping thunder
In the crowd, as a solo cowbell clangs out for gods.
Never mind Sunday sermons or church white spires.
Go ahead, raise your ink-stained arms of lightning.

Cymbals shiver and chaos grumbles as you dance
In time with congas and the kettle drums;
Remember when you had no sense of rhythm and
Could only see the Earth as blind? A wooden flute
Leaves a pretty scar floating across the village green.
Everywhere your feet feel the pulse of stone.

SIDEWALK GUITARS

Summer sculptures, air guitars,
Icons of the festival and ever since,
Displayed for tourists' sun-filled ears:
Everyone's favorite roar gone silent.

Wild amplifiers of youth's adrenaline,
Ambitions swung hard from their straps,
Loud and furious, polite as wood grain now.

Knowledge dumb without its finger pick.

Gods invented guitars for strutting on a stage:
Underground revolutions in three chords,
Idolatry in devastated hair and a scowl.
Tomorrow too late for anything that counts.
All the parties blazed until the end—a ukelele?

Rebellion died somewhere on this pretty
Sidewalk.

PRINT EXPRESS
AN ODE TO STREET POSTERS

Pirate communiqués for
Revolutionary means.

Instant access to chaos.
Nobody cancels the future.

Telephone pole manifestos
Enshrined by rusty stapling.

X-rated or general interest,
Philosophies endure in the rain.

Realistic excess or utopian restraint
Emboldened by next week's outbreaks.

Spare us your emergencies.
Save the world, instead.

GOLDEN NOTEBOOK

Get ready for the
Old-fashioned days when
Laughter began in the belly and
Drove both children and cockatiels to
Ecstasies uncharted by Freudians.
Never mind the Freudians.
Nobody important
Objects
These days to all the neuroses
Easily downloaded from the Internet.
Books are the devices that can slay you.
Once upon a time it was
Okay—and it still is—to
Kill time thinking dangerously.

CANDLESTOCK

Consolation's own pilot light.
An altar for a single pure thought.
Night pulls back into shadows to spy as
Drips draw rough spines down the wax sides.
Left alone, the flame might
Elope with the curtains, but not tonight.
Scholars have written scrolls by candlelight.
Trappists have chosen its truth over revolutions.
Once we tried to live by the stars, but learned we
Can't survive in the dark. A solitary
Knuckle of flame is our key.

LOTUS FINE ART

Lampshade glass
Overtures to savannas and
Tree frogs. Lampshade glass
Umbrellas of midnight white roses and
Southwestern lizards. Lampshade glass dragon-
Flies and peacock feathers fanning the sky.
In back, twelve varieties of glass souls.
Not one can't be shattered or cracked, but not one
Ever has, not by lovers or friends because we
Appreciate the art of glass stepping-stones.
Ruin has its own chapel up on the mountain.
The glass heart is the globe in your hands.

SHINDIG
DINNER WITH FRIENDS AFTER A DAY AT DIA:BEACON

So we eat dinner in pajamas, our new manifesto.

Here are the coins from our pockets, please take the buffalo.

I would praise Minimalism, but sculptors now sculpt everything with air.

Nobody appreciates a good sliding door like Dayl, our pony-tailed engineer.

Down in the basement the TV showed an artist walking in circles on his ceiling.

I don't know why every manifesto has failed before ours.

God has a purpose, but not on this menu.

YUM YUM

You
Understand
Mercy.
You
Understand
Mellow.
You may be
Undecided about
Machiavelli, but
You believe you can go
Unarmed out into the night.
May it be true for
You if
Unbelievable for anyone else.
Machiavelli ate noodles, too.

BLISS VS. EUPHORIA

Bastards can touch their toes. Angels can stretch their

Lips from sunrise to sunset in a smile, but

I bring a body to yoga as

Stiff as a pirate's plank I walk off and

Still can't find wisdom at the bottom of the sea. I'm a compendium of failed

Vows and funny

Socks. How do these women fold themselves into frogs

Emerging into boomerangs? The distance between my fingertips and my toes is like the

Upanishads, familiar to millions but vast and unknowable to me. I

Pretend to flow like a mountain stream. I pretend to be a

Heron balanced on a reed. I've voted for

Obama twice and petitioned against greed. Every woman in this room has no trouble

Resting her palms on the floor to feel the earth releasing inner peace—

I've got toes that cramp like angry children. My hamstrings

Are strung for war. Against what I haven't a clue.

MAVERICK FAMILY HEALTH

My toe is
All right. My
Veins have nothing to say. My
Esophagus is proud of its history. My
Right ventricle gets along with my left. My
Intestines have seen more than I care to remember. My
Cranium has been measured for both genius and intemperance. My
Knees will never be as limber as a child's, but my
Face gets better with age, and my
Asshole doesn't itch like it used to, thanks to your cream. Now
May
I be
Left in peace to
Yip and yowl and yell at the moon? My
Health needs an occasional night of insanity. My
Enthusiasm is dying of politeness on your padded table. My
Ambition has given enough blood at the lab. My
Lying cures more than you realize. My
Temper outranks your wall chart. May I ask if you remember
Heather, the nurse, who had such a way with a needle?

CVS

Center of nowhere
Vs.
Same as everywhere.

VIVIAN LETIZIA, DDS

Victory
Impossible in this chair.
Vice and its friends
Inevitable as gold fillings.
At least the new
Novocaine tastes like piña colada.
Lucky me, even if drooling, a lifetime of
Eating
Through sugary falsehoods
Iron-frowned
Zeus wouldn't have allowed.
Instant satisfaction always tops on my menu,
An all-American gourmet. The good
Dentist goes to work with her
Drill and her water
Spray. My tooth sings, a bionic mosquito.

HAIRCUTZ DAY SPA & SALON

Hell isn't big enough for her
Argument with hair. Don't think you're so
Innocent, either, hennaed, extended, and teased like
Rioting bird nests, you old disco queen. The Romans
Conquered empires for blondes, but in these cut-rate days
Utopians settle for dark roots and split ends galore. So don't dare go
Trump with your hair. Don't believe for a minute
Zsa Zsa Gabor is a look she'd sell you for all the monkeys in China.
Day spa, my
Ass.
You're parked in her chair for the capital treatment. May
She be merciful with your curls. She's at war with the first signs of
Plainness. God doesn't get to decide. Every woman needs a statement,
A few flaming streaks, a blowout worthy of empires.
& your eyebrows, what an emergency.
Slaves are no longer legal, but sure could help.
All the good ladies lie back in chairs with foam in their hair
Like aborigines engaged in the village ritual
Of cleansing grandmotherly worries from their hair.
Nobody remembers who invented the first bottle of hope.

MARTHA FRANKEL'S SUNGLASSES

Mars I'm not going to discuss. My
Astronaut didn't
Return with my slippers. But I say,
Thank
Heaven.
Am I not Queen of the
Frankels who love to gamble and gossip?
Romance is overrated twenty years into a mortgage. My
Agent can go write his own fucking screenplay. Awards are such
Nonsense. Give yourself the golden statue, as my mother always said:
Knaves and nincompoops now run the asylum,
Eastern religions won't solve the problem.
Last night Jack Nicholson called me to
Say nobody but your mother should see your true eyes:
Sunglasses are your ticket to glory. My
Underground friends all know
Nothing is cooler than Ray-Bans in basements:
Glamour can be yours merely by walking in the door. Your
Lazy days of bad-
Assing around are over now that you're blond.
Sunglasses can
Shield you from the blue-
Eyed devil at the next table
Stealing your soul. Here, take mine.

TACO JUAN'S BENCH

Taco Juan never walks by Taco Juan's, the bench wino said. Ain't no
Alhambra Jane in diamond pumps and ghost rider jeans, no
Cal City Caesar low riding low enough to scrape stars off the pavement.
Only me and a young hottie nursing an ice cream sat there to see
Jesus himself, like the original hippie, in American-flag
Underwear and dreadlocks and a belt cut from a rope.
All this Jesus did was pause at the bookstore window, gardening books on the left,
Nightstand books on the right, and finger his beard and pull out a tooth.
Sure enough, he dropped it in my beggar's cup when I wasn't really begging.
Bless him, but I'm twenty years past my last good smile and have a gap for the ladies. I
Earn my keep by waving bees off my orange drink and telling tourists from
New York I once went ten rounds with Rocky, and Thunderbird won.
Christ was an awfully nice guy, even if nobody saw him.
Hey, this tooth looks sorta like mine.

LETTERS TO THE EDITOR

Lilacs, latrines, letters to the
Editor, half of them longer than the Gettysburg Address and
Twice as important. Save Cooper Lake! Ban Corporate Greed. Oh, hell, Let
Teenagers Sleep Until Noon. Their Overpaid Teachers, too. Does the
Editor even read what he prints? The
Ranters hate the Truthers who hate the Birthers.
Save the Esopus! barely knows Save the Railroad! exists.
There's a whole page: Jay Wenk vs. Jay Wenk Has Finally Lost It.
Once I had plenty to say myself, decrying the spoilers and
The library haters and the fear that no one was listening. Now
Here I am, stumped by cruel fate: Why did the
Emerald Ash Borer kill my favorite tree? Why couldn't the
EMTs save Michael's dislocated shoulder from losing its nerves?
Don't answer with data. Don't wish me luck.
I plan to rant and rave until the moon has a black eye and
The sun burns its truth into everyone's skin.
Obituaries are the place to find kindness.
Really, the news never changes.

BUMPER STICKERS VS. BATHROOM GRAFFITI

Don't Drop Acid Just Take It Pass/Fail.
Don't Let Them Tame You. This is Bat Country.
What Happens in Woodstock Never Happens.
Better Than Bellevue. Still No Traffic Light.
Halfway House to the Real World. Send More Losers.
Please Don't Hit Me with that Crutch Hippy Beggarman.
If Evolution Is Outlawed Only Outlaws Will Evolve.
Your Reality Check Bounced. ET Phone Om.
If I Can't Dance It's Not My Revolution.
Fellow Pervert You're 40 Years Late.

ORIOLE 9 CHALKBOARD
"BEFORE I DIE I'D LIKE TO_____"

Okay, I'm the one who added *Eat an Elephant.*
Ride a Unicorn a little sweet, but I shouldn't say no.
"I contain multitudes," Whitman wrote, so should we all,
Our inner selves given orange chalk to rule the entryway hall:
Live a Little, Go to Disney for 100 Days, Have Sobriety,
Eat More Chalk, Cure F#cking Cancer, Do It!, Do Something Real.

9 lives are never enough.

Certainly, I could do more with my own,
Having spent almost a third of *Be 200* just being myself. *Go to*
Africa, See the Arctic Monkeys Perform, See the Taj Mahal,
Live 100 Days Without Fear, Be Rich, Have 100 Dogs.

Knowledge is fine,
But wouldn't you rather *Be a Stupid Monkey* or at least *Be the Ball*?

Okay, I'm not the one to *See Jack Hamm Naked* or *Eff My Dad's Best Friend,* but
Already I'm more open to *Make a Hole-in-One* or *Do a 5-Minute Yodel.*
Really, I should settle for *Be Warm* and *Publish My*
Damn Novel. Then *Marry Brittany* and *Sacrifice Goats.*

WOODSTOCK PUBLIC LIBRARY

Woofy, indifferent to poetry,
Otis, a spaniel always ready to roll over for a belly rub,
Olive, who should be in a movie as Lassie with a cowgirl's bandana,
Daisy, flat-out happiest napping under the reading table,
Sandra Dee, a dead ringer for her poodle owner minus the candy red glasses,
Tamar, parading her new buzz cut with loud nails on the linoleum;
Once Pepper chased a mouse from art books to fiction,
Chuckles was the one who chewed on old covers,
Kirk, so old his terrier beard looks one hundred and two.

Perhaps you've had the experience, browsing a paragraph of early
Updike in a crinkly plastic cover you have no intention of
Borrowing, of discovering a paw print on the page
Like a flashback to
Iron Jack, your panting husky, who
Came back from the stream to stand on the

Library book you'd left open on the picnic blanket;
Iron Jack, the idiot puppy, who then ate the
Bee in his food bowl for his first sting of knowledge.
Remember how he licked your lips to lick away the pain?
All the books you've read since then have shared those two feelings.
Right now your fingers can feel the grace of soft pages.
You carry a biscuit in your pocket for Rufus, who's waiting.

POST TRAUMATIC PRESS

Please don't let the dog out.
Okay, she'll be back. As I was
Saying
There's stress everywhere
These days. The community garden
Refuses to relocate,
And the community center is
Under renovation.
My friends in the peace movement
Act as if
The town council
Is their enemy, and I suppose a
Case could be made about the Memorial Day
Parade, but
Really I wish the dog would come back.
Easter isn't my favorite holiday.
Saturday is.
Saturday I plan to do nothing.

WDST

Why
Don't we
Strip to the
Temptations.
Why
Don't we
Sing karaoke to
The tempestuous twins.
Why
Don't we
Share
Tutti-fruiti
With our friends
Down at the
Sugar Shake Shack in
Tupelo-Tupeli,

Where
Donuts are free and
Sperm counts are strong.
The waiters and waitresses—
Wait, wait—
Don't press those buttons at home. Oops, this
Silence sounds like the dead zone.
Tomorrow
W
D
S
T
Will
Dedicate its
Soul of the week
To the First Church of Glee.

PAW

I

People have
Alleged
Woodstock is a
Pathetic refuge of
Arthritic barnyard realists and
Woebegone guitarists busking for
Pennies and plastic flowers.
All around you
Women hug their
Purses, and
Alimony is
Way past due.
Police
Arrest the
Whirlwind,

Panhandlers
Accost the
Weather, and
Psychiatrists
Annul your
Wallet.
Parody is on life support.
Asthma is the new
War cry of the
Perplexed.
Artists chew on
Wooden nickles, and
Paraphernalia
Always
Wanders off the reservation.

II

Performing
Arts of
Woodstock doesn't do
Purple
Allegories of
Wanton urchin lusts, or
Parables
Auguring
Widespread panic.
Performing
Arts of
Woodstock doesn't do
Paradox,
Acceptance, or
Wisdom of the ages.

Performing
Arts of
Woodstock
Prefers
Art stampedes and
Woozy warlock dances.
Puzzles left by
Alchemists have become our
Winter
Palaces.
Anarchy deserves its own raving
Whistle-stop.

|||

Please
Arrest your
Whiteness.
Please
Approve this message.
We
Prefer to be
Anonymous, but
We control the language. Our
P
A
W
Print is everywhere.
Angels can't escape us.
Writers get us in their heads.

Perhaps you've
Always
Wanted to say something new,
Purify your
Ambiguities or
Wrestle meaning to the floor. It's im-
Possible to get
Anywhere
Without us.
Pretend to be
Amazed.
We're sure to follow.

OUTDATED
POEM FOR A COFFEE CUP

Once you sat
Under
The tree of
Desire
All night
To taste the
Elusive
Difference.

BREAD ALONE

Brave and
Restless you
Eat candied hearts in
Apricot, prune, or cranberry.
Doom gives crunch to the oatmeal.
Alimony tastes like sourdough. Oh, you
Lonely warrior
Of the apocalypse, you claim the
Netherworld, but your secret fantasy is an
English breakfast with your mother's marmalade.

THE WOODSTOCK ROUNDTABLE

The revolution all
Hairy and
Ephemeral
Won't save you from the
Obvious or the
Obscure.
Don't
Sweat it, my friend.
Train wrecks are my middle name.
Occasionally, we
Can
Know the
Rest of the tragedy, but
Only
Under the strangest of circumstances when
Nobody
Dares to believe their own name.
Tell me everything
About your terrible needs, you
Beautiful
Little
Earthlings.

TO THE LETTER EXPUNGED FROM THE ALPHABET

America, I

Bought the

Chilies and

Donuts, the

Express train to

Freedom and

Go West Young Man. So

How am

I supposed to persuade the

Jury that we didn't

Know what would be

Lost? One

Morning

Nobody knew where to look.

Okay, we've

Petitioned and

Questioned and made our

Resolutions known.

Surely

This shouldn't be a mystery. Please

Understand, there are no

Villains here. So

Where did it go? Not

X

Y or

Z but the letter that filled the gap between you and me?

THE COMEAU PROPERTY
A TOWN PARK PASTORAL

There you go roving,

Heedless of dog walkers and Ultimate Frisbee.

Ecstasy

Comes easy under the blue sky.

On the summer Shakespeare stage a

Motorcycle gang performs "As You Like It" in leather. The

Easter egg hunt is still going strong in July.

A fawn stares like everything you do must be important and true.

Under the hemlocks you feel safe as a fairy tale:

Pileateds keep chipping away at casket holes, while

Red squirrels play at being a furious army. The stream spilling

Over the waterfalls is never bored by its own slap-happy monologues.

Perhaps heaven is a pirate ship cloud. Don't

Envy the field beyond the "No Trespassing" sign. The lonely

Rose-breasted grosbeak who spilled his heartbreak on-

To his chest needs

You to listen. Nothing is more naked than your ears at the Comeau.

SCARLET TANAGER

Sing your sore-throated robin's song
Claiming the upper branches of an oak tree.
All the times I've given my heart to your scarlet—
Remember? Your flying red kiss always too far from my
Lips. You flit in and out of sunlight, brilliant and drab,
Emotionally indifferent to my worship below,
Then dart off to your next perch, leaving
The vireo to sing its own off-note robin's song,
A languid complaint: *Here I am, where are you?*
Not here, not there, not after your scarlet rips
Away the solitary green comforts of my woods walk, the
Goodbyes I can't bring myself to say.
Every spring I savor my first scarlet sighting, a
Ravishing reminder of beauty too wounding to heal.

TIGER LILIES

Tawdry, open-throated glory cups begging for gallons of sticky July.
Insatiable pulpits of satin-dusted pistils and stamen gone wild from gardens.
Green wands spear-chucking their six-petaled hearts at the pollinators of chance.
Enduring pirates establishing outposts and empires in roadside waste spaces.
Rip-roaring colonies of braver-than-orange afternoon clusterfucks.

Lilies, you must know that deer will behead you, those
Insatiable cloven-hoofed Bambi rats of pastoral countrysides.
Lilies, you must know garden shears will cut you off at the throat
In demand for table arrangements both gloating and dying with excess,
Especially your burnt fringes and stout tongues. Lilies, speak loudly and
Speak strong, you're the crown rising out of the ditch's thicket of bones.

BLUEBIRDS

Blue-backed pickpockets of pretty days,
Liquid songsters, burblers,
Understudies to robins,
Emperors of field boxes.

Blue-backed but pugnacious as birds need to be,
Individualists on wires and fences,
Rivals to sparrows,
Diving into my heart with sky-stolen beauty.
See the red conquests on their chests before they fly.

PHOEBE

Perched on the wire, a dingy blunt apostrophe,
Honking your name, a permanent head cold.
Only you have the chutzpah to nest under my
Eave, an eyesore of straw leaking threads like a
Bowery bum, your gray coat grim as the thirties.
Enough is enough, you get to play Bogey in a poem.

ROADKILL RIP

Rabbit, don't do what you just did, not
On such a sunny blue Sunday. A soft thump, then
Another under my car, as the radio
DJ chides Mountain Jam fans for a hillside of litter.

Kindness sprinted out of the grass and
I killed it, just like the chipmunks and cat, the porcupine that
Lurched into my headlights, a tumbleweed
Lost between east bound and west. I

Remember them all, suicidal for my tires.
In an instant the day grows old.
Peace becomes carrion for the crows.

WAYWARD BALLOON

Wrapped around a pine sapling
A deflated silver lung

Yoked by twigs and needles
Wet in its slingshot pouch of rain.

All around, this forest must be a mile from any
Roads. Who might walk this way again?

Down on my knees, I untangle the
Blue ribbon that bent the sapling into

A supplicant, strangling the top. I
Let the whipsaw pine stand straight again.

Listen, we've launched satellites and probes to
Outer planets to search for the barest signs of life.

One balloon shouldn't prove the fallen state of man.
No, I pocket this shed skin, a token of modest deeds.

EMERALD ASH BORER

Eulogies, please, for
My ash cut down with such
Efficiency by the tree guy up in a bucket with a chainsaw and
Rope. Length by length he lowered the
Ash in orderly
Logs now stacked by the
Driveway. Oh, my noble natural flagpole, my
Ash once hugged by a bear and wrapped by a vine, what
Shall we do with so much sunlight baking the drive?
How naked you looked without leaves, how sullen. Your
Bare branches stabbed at the sky like rioting pitchforks. Sooner
Or later you would have dropped a dead limb on our car. You were no good as a
Ruin. You were a monument to the straight and the true now blighted by the
Emerald ash borers, tiny insects I never got to see. In the
Rain you'd smelled as green as first love, my ash, my native tree.

CASSIA BERMAN

Cassia, still with us on Facebook,
Are you? For a birthday? The
Spring peepers are
Shaking their sleigh bells
In the swamps. The daffodils
Are due any day. You had such a
Beautiful smile to go with your refusals: no
Ego, no hurry, no car, no wealth, no fear of death. I
Remember the raspberry pink rubber boots you wore for a
Marsh walk out to the lighthouse for a Valentine's Day poetry salon. The
Answer was always poetry. The question? Who can remember?
Namaste.

STILL STIRRING AT THE ARTISTS CEMETERY

MILTON AVERY

Milton, your nudes recline as stately as sand dunes, your moonlight does
Its dance on a black ocean. You, a shy bachelor nearly until forty.
Left to your own you would have remained a Sunday painter.
Then you married, simplified the sea and sky into hips and horizons.
Once you erased faces you let us see the souls of your women.
No one looked happier than your daughter reading a book on
An afternoon picnic, your true art form. I wish I could have lost my
Virginity in those dunes instead of on that college couch reeking of pot.
Emotional turmoil, my favorite pastime, found no room in your canvases.
Rage wasn't your style. You favored sailboats with billowing white breasts.
You're buried beside your wife who gave you your second life.

HERVEY WHITE

He only wanted his cot and his printing press.
Everything else was excess: the buccaneer festivals, the burning ship.
Rushed, always, he set the type before completing his verse.
Very few understood, his earlier novel had been lost in a warehouse inferno.
Everyone complimented his genius for friendship,
Yet he could only sell a few books.
Why does he seem so familiar?
Heating beans in a pot anyone could dip into.
Instead of the original hippie with a purple scarf for a belt
The true Hervey White was an ascetic racing against his fear of failure.
Everyone knew his poetry only grew worse with his efforts.

YASUO KUNIYOSHI

You painted alien-sized eyes and teaspoon plum lips on scarlet-clad women
All fleshy with thighs solid as milk pails yet hands small as a child's, all
Staring at a quiet thought somewhere to the left of your head. We
Understand, you couldn't become a citizen no matter how hard you tried.
Oval eggplant or yellow ladyslipper:
Kuniyoshi, you saw the curved power of women everywhere.
Undressed in shoulder-slipping negligé, they posed on a sofa or sat backstage,
Needing nothing more than brown light to be entertained.
I see the same face in all of them,
Yasuo, your mother? In a scarlet swimsuit she swims
Off the coast of Maine twice as large as the lighthouse island behind her.
She's trailing red hair and paddling with hands tiny as crabs, and
Here she is again, standing in the same black sea with an
Impossibly plump baby enthroned on her shoulders, big eyed as the clouds.

PHILIP GUSTON

Please, take off your hood, put down your brush & your bottle.
Hell, do you really need the solitary light bulb's hanging inquisition?
In the morning you're not the Klansman or the bloodshot cyclops you think you are.
Life should be more than a cigarette's chain gray accusation.
Instead of your studio as the pit of despair, try a still life without the Holocaust in mind.
Please, don't try to solve Richard Nixon by painting his jowls as pouchy as testicles.
Go ahead, go for a walk, get some greenery into your system.
Understand, your wife has her poetry, your daughter her friends.
Scruffy boot soles need not fill your paintings like the tombstones of kind thoughts.
Tomorrow won't make you more famous than today—not until after you're dead.
Once the sun sets, you return to mixing your palette for demons,
Never noticing the katydids outside your studio sawing their mysteries in half.

UPSTAIRS AT JOSHUA'S WITH SAUL

Upstairs with Saul, taking a-
Part poems like ripping the gift wrap,
Saul, who never tired of writing about the Flushing El or
The Marx Brothers, his
Antidote to a family history of sudden deaths. Saul,
I'll never forget your
Reverence for my drafts, your
Silence as if I'd hidden a koan in my latest
Account of my father's failures, this
Time in a potato-sack race when I was
Just a child at a county fair humiliated that my
Old man couldn't hop ten feet without
Stopping and fumbling with
His sack like a dress he couldn't hold up.
Upstairs with Saul, I could share
Anything in a poem, and if I
Succeeded, Saul
Would circle the last line and call
It a *real kick in the nuts*.
Then everything was worth it, the
Humbling of fathers and sons. Upstairs with
Saul I waited for his
Approval.
Upstairs, where I've now
Lost Saul for good.

FOR SALE WIN MORRISON

For starters, a glass cupola for my better angels. Then add
One dust-free attic for my ghosts to enjoy a happy
Retirement, plus a cedar closet for my magician's wardrobe.
Stone countertops for chopping my sorrows into
An arugula salad I'll someday serve to twenty.
Light fixtures to track my starry ideas.
East-facing windows for sex in the morning,
West-facing to say goodbye to the daily call for greatness.
Iron grates in the fireplace to burn my failed novel.
No basement because I gave it all to therapy.
Maybe French doors in case of a future wedding.
One rust-free padlock for the garden's ancient shed.
Room in the crawl space to pursue my second childhood,
Room under the cathedral ceiling to try on wings--
I'll take it all, plus Chinese whispers in the stream,
Sliding doors that open to my private forest,
One guilt-free night alone with the honey-varnished beams,
Nine bedrooms for the nine Muses before I burn the rocking chair.

THE STORIES BEHIND THE POEMS

Welcome to Woodstock
Paul McMahon produces the "Welcome to Woodstock" series of bumper stickers. He's also a musician who performs as the "Rock 'n' Roll Therapist." In his twenties he was in the art world. His work later appeared in "The Pictures Generation" show at the Metropolitan Museum. He's a quintessential Woodstocker of many talents. He also worked at the post office.

H. Houst & Son
As a Wasp, I share traits of the tribe, such as an inability to tell jokes. Here's the one I remember: How many Wasps to screw in a light bulb? Two: one to mix the martinis; one to call the electrician. Actually, I call my landlady, who even had to teach me how to pull the kitchen light cord (more gently) so that it works. So a hardware store is alien turf. Yet I love Houst. For a while, after a therapy session, I'd walk in, inspired by my therapist's account of Carl Jung, who took time from his workday to play like a child. I'd treat myself to helium balloons or hacky sacks, toys for my all-too-serious life.

Catskill Art & Office Supply
Music and art class in elementary school taught me that I couldn't sing or draw. No loss, really. I wanted to grow up to be a boxer or basketball player, a sportscaster at worst. Not until my thirties did I take a journaling workshop that taught me talent didn't matter; art supplies were for everyone. With a spray can of glue I added photos to my journals. Scissors led to collage making. Watercolors looked joyous with my childlike squiggles. Finger paints let me be an Abstract Expressionist. Catskill Art & Office Supply keeps offering invitations to try new things. But I still can't sing.

Marilyn Crispell
Marilyn Crispell trained in classical piano. At twenty-eight, she heard John Coltrane's *A Love Supreme* emerge from stereo speakers like a living force that changed her life. She become an improvisational pianist and moved to Woodstock in 1977 to join the Creative Music Studio that hosted musicians from around the world. Typically, I've driven to Manhattan to hear her perform with jazz greats like Gary Peacock or Paul Motion, but once or twice a year she plays in Woodstock. Don't miss her.

Michael Perkins, Poet

Michael Perkins began writing poems as a fourteen-year-old in Dayton, Ohio in the fifties, where he soon won a city-wide contest that gave him the confidence to continue for a lifetime. In the sixties he moved to the East Village and opened a bookstore, which introduced him to the Beats and other hipsters, but his own poetry remained defiantly classical in spirit. He has told me not to write poetry for acclaim. Instead, he has quoted Sam Hamill: "Poetry is not commerce. It is not something to be exchanged or traded. It is a gift to the poet, a gift for which the poet, eternally grateful, spends a lifetime in preparation, and which the poet, in turn, gives away and gives away again."

Mikhail Horowitz

Since 1986, Mikhail Horowitz has been the speaking half—boy, does he speak—of a comedic duo with Gilles Malkine that brings the Marx Brothers spirit to *The Norton Anthology*. They sing, they rap, they abuse Samuel Beckett. In his other life as a serious person, Mik writes inventive poetry that makes my acrostics look like child's play.

Sparrow

Once renowned as an East Village poet, Sparrow is now renowned as a Phoenicia poet. He actually did run for President, mainly, I suspect, to write an endearing essay about his crusade for *The Sun*. Always up for a challenge, he replied with a "Will Nixon" poem:

BY THE TIME YOU GET TO WOODSTOCK

Wandering through the town of Woodstock
In the scenic Catskill Mountains,
Looking for souvenirs,
Looking for the exact spot where Janice Joplin shout-screamed "Piece of My Heart" in 1969,

"No, that wasn't here,"
Insensitive locals will tell you.
"X that off your list
Of Historic Localities.
Nothing much ever happened here."

Colony Café

Built in 1929 as way station for guests on their way up to the hotel on Overlook Mountain, the Colony has a checkered history. For years, the owner, an antiques enthusiast, used it as a private warehouse. In 2000, new owners revived it as a performance space. Phillip Levine began hosting poetry open mics on Monday nights that brought out the poets, the crazies, and perhaps a genius or two. He believed in giving everyone a fair chance. The series continued until 2008. He now runs the Woodstock Poetry Society.

Your Box of Crayons

In 2014 the Shandaken Theatrical Society presented *The Lady in Question,* an adoring spoof of a World War II damsel-in-distress movie. Charles Busch, the playwright, had originally performed the role as a comic transvestite. To help the actor develop his/her role as the Lady, director Gordon Brown told him to use his box of crayons.

Donald Fagen, Asshole

Donald Fagen is the singing half of the duo behind Steely Dan, the band that provided the soundtrack to my college years in the late seventies. At halftimes our marching band belted out a big brassy version of "My Old School," one of Steely Dan's classic takes on the soured sixties.

Beware of your idols. In a "Walking Woodstock" column for the *Woodstock Times* about the Byrdcliffe colony, I recounted the story of Bob Dylan's stay in a historic house, where he felt invaded by kooks from across the country searching for the Prince of Protest. I added that another rock star lived in the place now, enjoying a more genteel existence. A week later a letter to the editor savagely attacked me and my colleague, Michael Perkins, as money-grubbing, celebrity-stalking, tabloid scum, or words to that effect. It had been written by Donald Fagen's wife. Michael fired back with a letter challenging her to a duel by water pistol. Then Donald Fagen weighed in, stern but grumpy, defending his wife and his good name as a musician. A coward at heart, I've waited years to join the fray. Revenge is sweet, but, truth be told, listening to Steely Dan is sweeter.

The Center for Photography

In the sixties, the Center for Photography at Woodstock building was the Café Espresso, a Greenwich Village-style bistro. The young owners, Mary Lou and Bernard Paturel, welcomed an even younger Bob Dylan like an extended member of the family. He had an upstairs writing studio in a room that otherwise held a workbench.

Michael Lang, Music Promoter
In his twenties Michael Lang was one of the four organizers of the Woodstock Festival, the one who expressed its entrepreneurial hippie spirit. He went on to manage Joe Cocker, Rickie Lee Jones, and others. His book, *The Road to Woodstock,* is great fun to read.

Tinker Street Cinema
Built in 1832 as a Methodist church, the structure was converted to a movie theater in 1967. I googled a recording of Jimi Hendrix jamming at the theater a week before the Woodstock Festival. It sounded terrible.

At Levon's Grave
Levon Helm played drums for The Band. By middle age, he was a beloved figure in Woodstock. After being treated for throat cancer, he began raising money to cover his medical bills by hosting Midnight Rambles at his home studio, "The Barn," which featured a house band and many guests over the years. I had the good fortune to attend a show not long before he died in April 2012.

Cooper Lake
Cooper Lake, the Kingston reservoir, was a pond before dams enlarged its size. More people may have believed an April Fools' Day story published in the *Woodstock Times* about the discovery of a Viking ship's remains on its shoreline than have accepted my claim of a whale lurking under its placid surface, but I refuse to accept reality without a fight.

Chainsaw Bear
Robert Wyatt, a retired book editor with 20,000 volumes in his rustic home, has a chainsaw bear on his deck named "Amanuensis," who sends me e-mails. To return the kindness, I wrote a poem. His name, for those like me who didn't know the word "amanuensis," refers to someone who takes dictation or copies a manuscript.

fiberflame
An arts and crafts studio in an exotic metal-box building outside of town, fiberflame is an invitation to a second childhood. I've made picture frames and a glazed mug, but nothing to rival the Cy Twombly-like swirls on a dinner plate produced by a three-year-old at the next table.

Print Express

Print Express prints and distributes posters for many of the cultural institutions in our region promoting concerts, plays, and events. Why not a poem? From my series inspired by *Night of the Living Dead*, I chose "Child Star," a poem about the zombie girl who digs the heart out of her mother's chest with a trowel. Did my poster cause a stir? No. It vanished like yesterday's newspapers.

Golden Notebook

In 1978 co-founder Ellen Shapiro named her bookstore The Golden Notebook after a Doris Lessing novel.

Shindig

Dia:Beacon is a mecca of Minimalist art, a converted factory in which a gallery may hold nothing more than a pile of broken mirror glass or a few strings strung between the ceiling and floor. Sometimes I've finished my visit in twenty minutes, feeling dismissive. On better occasions I've left with the belief that anything can be enchanting if approached with wonder.

Yum Yum

Yum Yum is a noodle bar.

Bliss vs. Euphoria

Laura Weiss, my yoga teacher, has tried and tried. Bless her. I began taking her class at Bliss Yoga, but after a few years she and several other teachers left to start Euphoria Yoga. Only in Woodstock, I thought, could the yoga business go the way of McDonald's vs. Burger King, CVS vs. Rite Aid, etc. The new venue had creakier floors, but Laura's enthusiasm never wavered.

CVS

CVS originally stood for Consumer Value Stores. Launched in Lowell, Massachusetts in 1963, the chain reached Woodstock in 2001, generating controversy by replacing the town's last supermarket. "Food, Not Drugs," said one picket sign. "Community Need, Not Corporate Greed," said another. Explaining the outrage, supervisor Jeremy Wilber told *The New York Times*, "Woodstock cannot be crucified on the cross of CVS." But the pharmacy opened, and life went on.

Haircutz Day Spa & Salon
After giving a copy of *The Pocket Guide to Woodstock* to the owner of Haircutz Day Spa & Salon in hopes that she might sell copies to the ladies browsing magazines while seated for hair treatments, I returned several days later to find her furious that her salon hadn't been mentioned in the guide. New book. Wish granted.

Martha Frankel's Sunglasses
The indomitable Martha Frankel spearheads the Woodstock Writers Festival. As a magazine journalist, she profiled celebrities. *Hats and Eyeglasses* is her memoir about her childhood family's love for gambling.

Bumper Stickers vs. Bathroom Graffiti
Paul McMahon has produced dozens of punchlines for his "Welcome to Woodstock" bumper stickers. In Oriole 9 the bathroom graffiti includes both quotes from the likes of Truman Capote and comments from anonymous quipsters. I made a mashup from both sources.

Oriole 9 Chalkboard
An artist in New Orleans, Candy Chang, established the first "Before I die I want to____" chalkboard on the wall of an abandoned building after losing a friend. The idea spread to more than seventy countries and to the Oriole 9 restaurant entryway.

Woodstock Public Library
In 2009 the library produced a Dogs of the Library calendar that inspired this poem.

Post Traumatic Press
Dayl Wise started Post Traumatic Press in 2000 with the help of his wife Alison Koffler to publish works by veterans. They expanded to publish local poets as well, including a chapbook of mine, *My Clone*. Nearly everyone who opens the cover in my presence smiles and asks, "What is Post Traumatic Press?"

PAW
Founded in 1964, Performing Arts of Woodstock prides itself on presenting serious dramas rather than the familiar chestnuts of community theater.

Outdated

One of my fantasies has been to publish a poem on a coffee cup. So I was in luck when I brought my visiting cousin and nephew to breakfast at Outdated: An Antique Café in Kingston. A contest flier by the cash register invited us to fill in a small box with an illustration to be used on an Outdated travel mug. We ignored the box, but collaborated on an acrostic poem for "Outdated." I don't remember what we wrote, but we did use "dirty/Underwear" for the "U" line. We felt so inspired that we read our potential prize winner aloud to the bearded cashier. He had the pained smile of a guy thinking, "What did I do to deserve this?"

We didn't win. Days later Facebook revealed the chosen illustration to be what I'd describe as a sci-fi variation on a deep-sea diver's helmet. Being a lawyer, my cousin fulminated over our loss by e-mail, but, as a poet who has lost many contests (and won a few), I reminded him that there's no accounting for taste. Then I wrote this short version of "Outdated" that could actually fit on a cup.

The Woodstock Roundtable

Doug Grunther hosts the Sunday morning Woodstock Roundtable on WDST, a show that might feature an interview with a psychic followed by one with a United States congressman. For a time, my friend, Saul Bennett, a retired PR executive, invited local writers to join him for poetry segments on the show. After his death, I filled his role for several years.

The Comeau Property

Originally a private estate near the heart of the village, the Comeau Property was bought by the town in 1979. The house became the Woodstock Town Hall. The grounds have soccer fields, an outdoor stage for the Bird-On-A-Cliff Theater Company to perform Shakespeare, and woodland trails that lead alongside the Sawkill.

Emerald Ash Borer

In the fall of 2012 I returned from two months away to discover that every ash tree in the neighborhood had been "blonded," or stripped, of its bark by woodpeckers digging for the larva of emerald ash borers, an invasive beetle from Asia.

Cassia Berman

Cassia Berman left us in 2012, a shock because she still seemed young even with her poodle gray curls. She died within weeks of being diagnosed with a fatal illness, terrible news that she'd shared with close friends without feeling terrible herself. A true Woodstock spirit, she was a Qigong teacher, a library trustee, a poet, and a woman who always needed a ride to events because she didn't drive.

Still Stirring at the Artists Cemetery

In 1934, the Kingsbury family buried a teenage son, who'd been killed in a car accident, under a small memorial boulder near the top of a grassy rise. They didn't intend to establish an artists' cemetery—in fact, locals initially disparaged the place as the "artists'" cemetery—but major figures from the arts colony chose the same burial grounds, a tradition that continues to this day.

Whenever I visit, I think of a passage in Walt Whitman's *Leaves of Grass* in which he described grass as "the beautiful uncut hair of graves." He also called grass "the flag of my disposition, out of hopeful green stuff woven." I always leave the artists' cemetery inspired to get back to work.

Milton Avery

Not until he was nearly forty did Milton Avery meet his younger wife, Sally, who enabled him to move to New York City in 1925 to pursue art full time. Until then, he'd lived in Hartford and held clerical or blue-collar jobs to support his ambition to paint. In New York he learned Modernist techniques that led him to flatten and simplify images while heightening the colors. Unlike his younger colleagues, Adolph Gottlieb and Mark Rothko, he never shifted into pure abstraction. For decades, the Averys summered in Maine, Vermont, or Cape Cod. They didn't arrive in Woodstock until 1950, but they chose to be buried here.

Hervey White

Hervey White arrived from Chicago as an assistant to Ralph Radcliffe Whitehead, the wealthy English founder of the Byrdcliffe colony, in 1902. After several years, White left to buy an old farm across the valley, which gradually became the Maverick, still the home for an open-air music hall that has hosted chamber music for a century. From 1915 until 1931, the Maverick held festivals under the full moon in August. Attendees were invited to dress as gypsies or whatever the year's theme might be. One festival ended with the burning of a wooden ship. Michael Lang knew of this history when he conceived of his Woodstock Music & Art Fair held in 1969.

In Chicago, White had early success as a novelist. Theodore Dreiser called his second book, one of the six "great novels of the world." But after the inventory for these books was lost in a warehouse fire, he "lost faith in trade publishers," as Alf Evers wrote in *Woodstock: History of a Small Town*, and started his own press to publish himself and others. In Woodstock, White felt more highly regarded as a cultural promoter than as a writer.

Yasuo Kuniyoshi

Yasuo Kuniyoshi arrived in Seattle from Japan at the age of sixteen in 1906, but was never able to gain United States citizenship before dying in 1953. As a young man, he made his way to the Art Students League in Manhattan, where he met his first wife and later taught for many years. In 1929, he built a summer house in Woodstock. He became one of the preeminent painters of his day. In 1948, he was the first living artist given a retrospective at the Whitney Museum of American Art. In 2015, the Smithsonian American Art Museum revived his reputation with an exhibition curated by Tom Wolf, a Bard professor and scholar of the Woodstock Arts Colony.

Philip Guston

Philip Guston first visited Woodstock in the early forties, then bought an artist's studio in the Maverick in 1948. He had a long and distinguished career as both a painter and a teacher. In the thirties, he started out as a muralist for the WPA. By the fifties he was an Abstract Expressionist whose pink and white brush strokes remind me of fallen cherry blossoms. In 1970, he made a radical break. Not only did he return to figurative painting, but he drew cartoonish Klansmen, which led critics to claim that his fine art sensibilities had been been corrupted by the rage of the sixties. For the remaining decade of his life, he devoted himself to painting in his Woodstock studio and befriending poets. Today, his late paintings are seen as a turning point in American art from abstraction to personal imagery.

Upstairs at Joshua's with Saul

My dear friend and poetry mentor, Saul Bennett, and I spent long afternoons sharing our poems. He sat for so long absorbing my drafts in silence before commenting that I couldn't help but believe that every word deserved to be as strong as possible. He was the best kind of editor, enthusiastic about my talents but unabashed with his pen. If he circled the last line and called it "a real kick in the nuts," I knew the poem had succeeded. If he drew a line across the middle to call the piece "a twofer," I knew the weak half needed to be overhauled to stand on its own as a poem.

Usually, we met in our homes, but one Thursday when his driveway was being repaved, we sat upstairs at Joshua's. After critiquing poems, we relaxed and shared a laugh over an episode in his life that seemed like a scene from his beloved Marx Brothers. He'd fainted at the library, which had led him to take medical tests that found him to be in good health. Returning to the library to thank them for reacting to his collapse with professionalism, he'd promptly fainted again. This coincidence struck us as hilarious, as if Saul had suffered a psychosomatic reaction to the library worthy of a comedian.

Afterward, we parted on the sidewalk. "Next time, we'll meet at my house," he called out. His driveway would be ready. I never anticipated that those would be his last words to me. Sunday evening he died of a heart attack.

Every so often, I'm lucky to dream about Saul. I wake up with renewed faith in my poetry. Not until middle age had he begun writing poems, "shocked" into this life-saving pursuit, as he said, by the sudden death of his oldest daughter. Here's one of his late poems:

SAMARITAN ON A BRIDGE

Poetry came for me
late. It led me
off the bridge. It showed me
home when it, not I,
knew where home was.
It stayed up reading
my blood, hectoring
my soul. I felt enrolled
in its gospel
of submission.